Going through the motions

Kayden Hamlin

 BookLeaf Publishing

Presentation by *BookLeaf Publishing*

Web: www.bookleafpub.com

E-mail: info@bookleafpub.com

ISBN: 9789357747714

First edition 2023

You pick up a book and flip to the dedication, only to find the names of people unknown to you. Only this time, it's different. We may not have met, maybe not in person, but by the time you've read and finished this book, our souls will be a bit more familiar with one another.

So to my wonderful readers: I would like to thank you for taking the time to read the words of my soul, and I hope this book finds you well.

To my family, who has always loved and supported me and for being my muse. For you have all instilled in me a desire to do good and to be the good in this world and to be the best and most genuine version of myself.

To my friends, who have stuck by my side and supported me from the beginning. Your love has helped to carry me this far.

To those who have inspired any of these pieces written here before you, some strangers and some not, your souls will forever live on within these pages.

To my beautiful angels watching over me from above, may you rest easy.

To my God, my Father up in heaven, for blessing me with the ability to share my passion

words of the soul

when you read the words written here on this
page, you're looking so much deeper than you'll
ever realize

for these words were once thoughts that were
left unspoken

thoughts that once and perhaps still do weigh on
my mind as if the crushing weight of the world
was on my shoulders

when you read my words, you are slowly
unraveling the invisible shackles that once left
me entangled

you feel what i have felt

when you read my words, you get an
understanding of the intensity that lingers within
me, within my mind, soul, and spirit, and that
slowly pours out onto the page like spilled ink

when you read my words, you are getting a good
look into my soul

i write these words that speak to me
my goal is to make you feel
and sometimes
that's all we've ever really needed
to simply feel

projection

i used to say that i hated when it stormed
that when it did, my depression came out to play,
and every bone in my body shook
it was weird
how it all worked
i could never really explain it myself

but somewhere down the line, i've seen the
similarities between myself and each drop of
rain that pelts down, leaving a familiar sting to
the skin

the way the thunder crashes and cries acts as a
reminder of how i am internally screaming, and
every time i jump from fear, it reminds me of
how i am exhausted from this feeling of
lonesome seclusion

the lightning lights up the sky leaving behind
exquisite colors and painting the sky with
different patterns

but even i know that all things beautiful still
come with their share of chaos

so maybe it's not the storms i'm afraid of but
rather the similarities seen between them and me

perhaps it's the storm of my past and present that
crash into a loud thunder that scares me the most

so if this fear and hatred has only been yet
another projection, then i wish to apologize to
the sky, for i have always loved your beauty

and somewhere down the line forgot that that
includes your storms too

- please accept my sincerest apologies

waves

could you imagine going about your everyday
life and then randomly, out of nowhere, a wave
crashes into you

could you imagine coming up for air gasping,
struggling to stay afloat just to be knocked down
again and again, wave after wave

after a while, you think the storm has cleared
and think to yourself

"i'm safe now; it's over, i made it"

but as soon as you allow yourself to get happy at
the thought, another wave comes crashing even
harder than the one before it

your chest gets tight

you want to feel safe and to make things go back
to normal, but with every attempt, another wave
comes crashing, dragging you down deeper and
deeper until it feels like you're drowning

now i want you to imagine how that would feel
as everyone else around you continues about
their day as if nothing is happening

as you're gasping for air and struggling to stay
strong, people walk right past you as if
everything is okay. they can't see those waves
that are dragging you down; they can't see how
you're slowly sinking deeper and deeper

you can try to scream for help, but the water has
already filled your lungs, as you've suddenly
gone mute
could you imagine how that'd feel
because that's my life

these demons in my head cause this
never-ending sadness, and that sadness comes in
waves

every time i think i've gotten better, it comes
back even more potent, crashing into me as i
sink deeper and deeper into my own self agony

i go about my day as if nothing's happening, just
as you do yours, but what you can't see is that
i'm drowning in these waves that only i can feel,
and my thoughts act as ropes leaving me
entangled with no way out

you see me, and you see my smile
you hear me as i laugh and joke
but underneath the surface, i've lost
consciousness, and i no longer feel in control

the waves crash into me, making me feel like i
could die, yet each time they come and go, i
remain alive, and the same thought plays
through my head

i wish i were dead
i wish the waves would stop, and when they
don't, i hope they'd finally take me
i try to learn to surf, but the waves swallow me
whole
i guess i can't complain too much because
everyone seems to leave

but this sadness always seems to find its way
back to me as if its familiarity invites me in with
open arms

and i've learned that feeling that sad is better
than feeling nothing at all

i am lonely

i am lonely

and i am so tired of feeling alone
as if i'm always the last choice

the one they come to when it's beneficial for
them, but otherwise, i am left on the top shelf

collecting dust, i sit here patiently waiting with
my thoughts in solitude

i question why i am not good enough

why i have never been cared for or loved the
way that i love
but loving is just who i am and who i always
was

 i question my own worth

or why i'm good enough to help their image but
not good enough to keep around

like i am nothing but decorative

merely a nick-nack stored away
the not so fine china on display
but in reality, i am as flimsy as a paper plate

i am lonely

i am a sense of lonely that sits with you for a
while
that lingers in your stomach, your chest, and
your throat, and that suddenly makes you choke
on your own words

i am a sense of lonely that hits you with such
intensity that you question if you've ever
actually had anyone at all

lonely doesn't even begin to explain this feeling

i believe it would be too easy for me to say that i
was invisible

maybe part of me wishes it were true

because the painful fact is that i am very much
visible, but no one has ever put in much effort

they pile me away in boxes until they feel as
though i'll be useful and then a trophy i will be

yet again on display for everyone to see

only i have always been more of the second
place and never the first

i am only the participation award

i'll sit there quietly with a smile on my face as i
convince myself they care, but when reality hits,
it always hits hard

i am still left feeling lonely
even in a crowded room

i am lonely

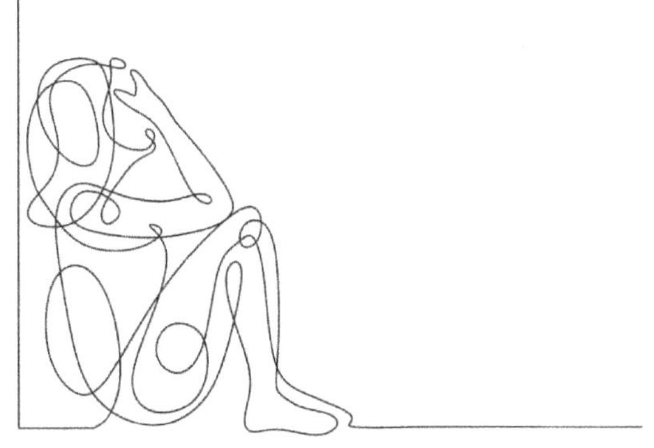

lifelines and warning signs

and i feel as if i'm at a constant war between
choosing my happiness over my health

as if choosing them both is no longer an option
as if both decisions come with a punishment and
a reward

you see when i eat, i am healthy

more motivation
more energy
never having to worry about the concern or
questions from others

but when i see the number go down, i suddenly
have a sense of fulfillment, and even if it be an
illusion, i am content within my own
self-destruction

who knew that a key to survival could also act as
a reason to no longer wish to survive

- i guess you can't have your cake and eat it too

~

i may not relate to this now, but a past version of
myself once did, and so i dedicate this to her and
to those who may also relate. may you realize
that you are never as alone as you may feel, and
may your heart be filled with self-love.

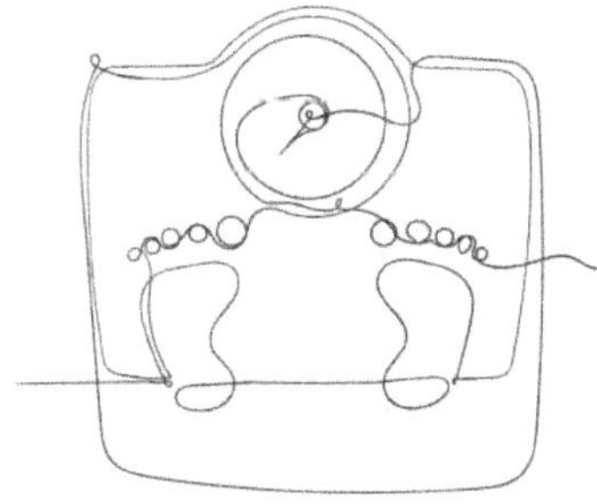

leaky faucet

my mind is like a leaky faucet
a drip here
a drip there
a thought here
and a thought there
and eventually, i'm left with a puddle

only this puddle isn't merely a puddle but instead
a puddle so vast that i feel as if i could drown at
any moment

the thoughts come and go in waves

the demons i face on a daily basis leave me with
self-doubt and insecurities that pile up like dirty
dishes

they sit there waiting to be put away, but i never
have the motivation nor the will to conquer them
head-on as if it's a chore in itself to simply feel
them in the first place

but maybe the dripping isn't so bad, those
thoughts that continue to spill out

because they distract me from the silence and
sadness is the loudest silence i have ever heard

i tell myself it's all in my head but that is
precisely the problem

my mind is like a leaky faucet

to my younger self

if i could talk to any person, dead or alive, who
would it be

you ask me this question and expect it to be
easy, but i respond with i don't know

the truth is i'd pick my younger self

i'd hold her tightly and tell her i'm sorry,
knowing there's no preparation for what's to
come

i'd remind her that she's not a burden or
worthless and that not everything is her fault

i'd tell her it's not her job to carry the weight all
alone and to focus on being a kid, although i
know she wouldn't listen

after all, she is me, and i was once her and i
know how important protecting those around her
always was and still continues to be

i'd tell her she's beautiful and more than enough,
even despite the horrible things she'll be told
growing up

i'd remind her that her body is her own and to
protect it at all costs and that feeling is the only
way to heal

i'd cry as i think of all the things she'll endure as
those around her neglect every experience and
emotion she felt

they'll say she's too young, but even she'll know
that that is precisely the problem

she was too young to have gone through so
much

i'd try to remind her to speak up because i
remember how i never did, and i now live with
those memories forever taunting me and me
alone

not a single soul knowing the true extent of what
that little girl and i have been through

i'd tell her how brave she is and to stop putting
so much pressure on herself

to live life with laughter and that i still admire
how, despite everything she's been through, she
still has such a big heart with more than enough
love for anyone and everyone she encounters

i'd take her by the hand and explain that
although she'll go through some pretty horrible
things and although i'm still unsure of what's to
come, where we are now is a place we once
prayed and pleaded to god for

we can say we made it, and we did it on our own
but how would i explain all of this to an outsider
looking in
such fear i'd have of the judgment i would get
so i'll stick with my original
"i don't know"
while i continue to pray for and heal my younger
self

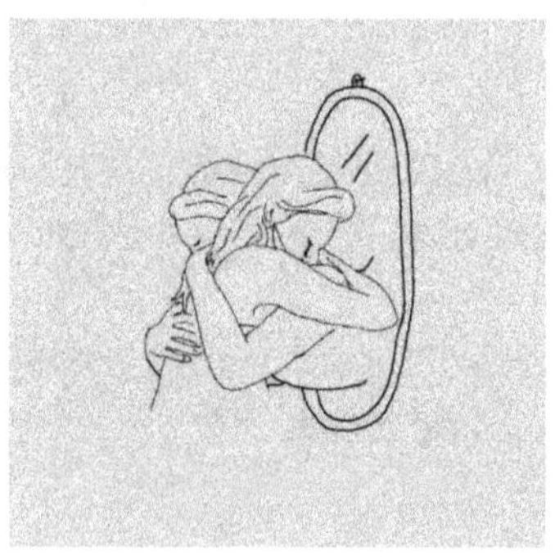

pain in love

my dad always told me that i was too young to
know what love really was
but when i saw you smiling at another
i thought to myself

i may not know what love is
but i do know pain
and this
this is pretty damn painful

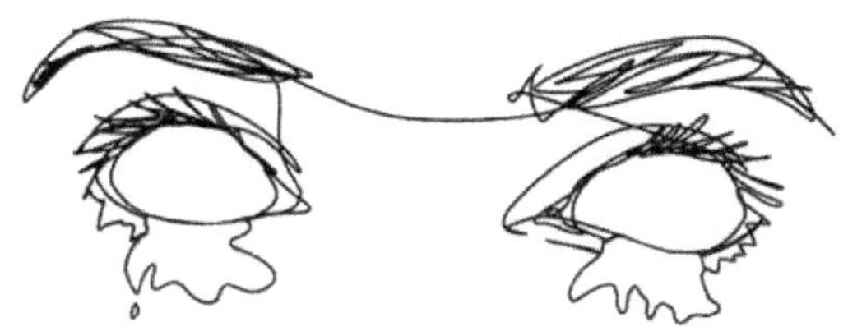

divorce is never easy, especially not for the kids

my heart wants to be home
it aches for a place i'm not even sure exists
i lost my home long ago when my family went
from being whole
to being completely broken
to being split
now i'm just living within these walls that
suffocate me as i stare at them with the same
empty and emotionless expression every night
now i am only living under a simple roof

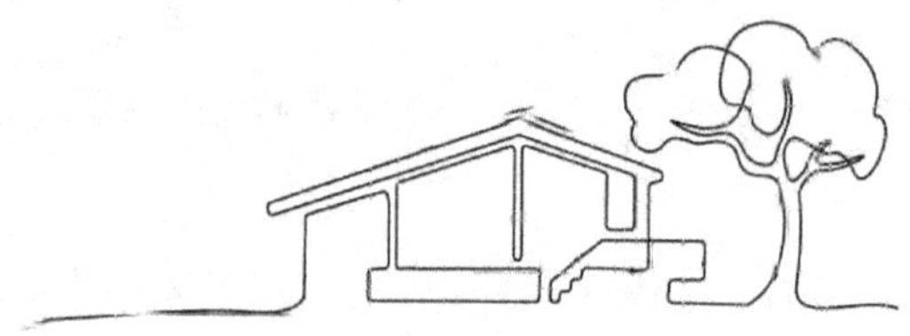

homesick

if you feel as if you're homesick
homesick for a place that you've never been and
not even sure exists
i'll take you by the hand in hopes to get there
together
a place for you to call and to feel at home
and maybe,
just maybe
you'll find that place in me
maybe, just maybe
we'll find that place in each other

my nothing

i tell myself to never settle
but i find myself settling to miss you

i suppose it's the best i can do at this time

to reminisce on memories that once was
going over the what-ifs and the maybes

and i know that i should want better than that but
if better means anything other than you then
better isn't something that i want

i suppose it's true what they say,
that nothing lasts forever

but if nothing lasts forever then i wish my
nothing would have been you

holding on to nothing

someone once told me that i needed to heal my
heart
i jumped up and screamed no
because in my eyes
healing means that i have to let you go
and that is something that i never want to do

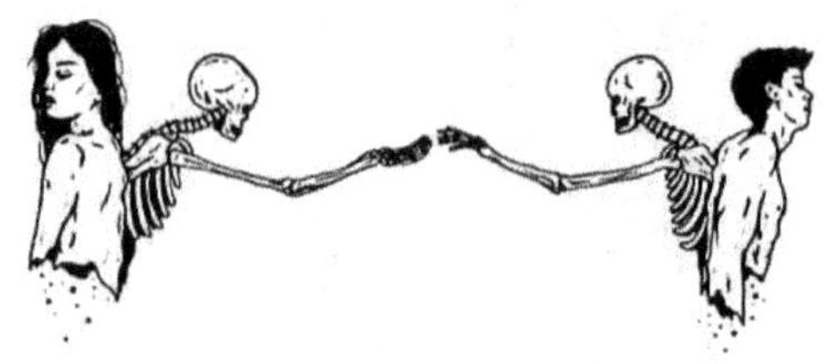

the neverending poem

you

and suddenly, the most beautiful poem has just
been made

you

you are my poem

you are my love, my passion, my everything,
and like my love for you, this poem can only
grow

'you' turns into 'your'

and 'your' turns into

your smile

your eyes

your voice

your laugh

your humor

your expressions

your passion

your presence

you

and suddenly, just like that, you're all i can ever
think of

my first thought in the morning, and my last
thought at night. the one i want in the middle of
the day on a quiet afternoon when my mind is
already occupied but i'd still rather be
experiencing life with you

william shakespeare once said

"love comforteth like sunshine after rain"

well, you are my sun

the comfort after the rain

you are my moon on my dark days

i once read a quote that explained driving on a
stormy day. how when you're driving under a
bridge and suddenly everything stops.
everything goes silent and suddenly seems
peaceful. you finally get out, and everything hits
you a little harder than before

you are my bridge

you are the face i hope to see as i pass all of
those people walking aimlessly on those
unfamiliar streets

the ones i walked at night in hopes of finding
some sort of distraction

your image appears on the walls of my bedroom
as i lay there at night staring at them with the
same blank and emotionless expression on my
face

tears slowly falling as i recollect every memory
of you, and i

whether they be little, brief, long, good, or bad,
and i hold onto them like my life depends on it

the thought of having you is a blessing, but it is
a blessing that can kill, just like the dreams i
have because somehow they are all filled with
you

i don't know what is worse

knowing that you have taken over my dreams or
knowing that at some point, i have to wake up
knowing that you will never be mine

and that is when i realized that the poem is a
never-ending cycle

it never intended to stop at all of those amazing
things because "you' can also lead to

you never chose me

you don't even know who i am

you chose her

you'll never know

you and i didn't work out

you will never be mine

you used me

you took advantage of me

you broke me

 you

grief is just love with nowhere to go

i am happy
even though i am in pain

i am happy
that it hurts so fiercely as i grieve the loss of
your presence

i am happy
that my chest gets tight and my vision blurs as i
reminisce the moments we once shared and the
memories that i cling to

and even though this pain hits me with such
intensity

i am happy
and i am thankful
to have had someone like you
that had made such an impact on my life to have
caused saying goodbye to be this excruciating

a letter to my siblings

as i look into your eyes, it's like you bring life into my lungs and inspire me to breathe

i take a deep breath as i take in your beauty and innocence

your purity and contentedness in life

you constantly remind me that the little things aren't as little and simple as they may appear

if inspiration had a face, i feel as though i'd see it in each of yours

you all inspire me to live life with purpose and push the boundaries of what is possible

through your eyes, you may seem ordinary, but it's the originality of your souls that i admire

life is unpredictable, and i may not be able to protect you from everything but let this be my promise to you that you'll never go through anything alone

when you look into the mirror, i hope that you
love the person staring back at you

that you never pull back your tides in fear of
being too much because i love everything that
you are and everything that i know you'll one
day be

may you never lower your voices, and may you
forever stand your ground

know that you have a concrete voice
and when you speak, i hope you speak loud and
proud

remember that growth isn't linear and that
having a good day isn't as important as simply
having one

when hard times come, let my words act as your
reminders

repeat these words over again and come to me
whenever you're seeking shelter

you are strong
you are independent
you will make it
you are smart

you are loved
and you have always and will always be enough

emotional intimacy

i think there's something so beautiful about
emotional intimacy

something so pure
something that holds so much importance

like yes,
open up to me and show me the parts of yourself
that often hide in the dark

you say your mind is like a long and dark
hallway, but i've always been fascinated by the
darkness, so let me open up those curtains and
tear down your walls

i'd let the light shine in every dark corner you're
used to hiding in

tell me your passions, your hopes, and your
dreams

let me support you through anything and
everything that life throws your way

i don't just want to know your favorite color or
your favorite food

i want to build a connection and get a good look
into your soul

i want to know that your favorite color is yellow
because it reminds you of the sun on a rainy day
or how your favorite food is homemade soup
because your mom made it for you every night
that you were sick, and it reminds you of home

i'll tell you my favorite book, and i'll read to
you each line

i'll listen to your stories, and don't you dare be
afraid to cry

because hell, we all need a good cry sometimes

tell me the story of how you became the person
you are today

tell me about all of the heartbreaks
the good days
and everything in between

and i will hold onto each word as if my life
depends on it

i promise to touch your soul before i ever dare to
touch your body

and if you understand the importance of those
words, then you, my dear, are golden

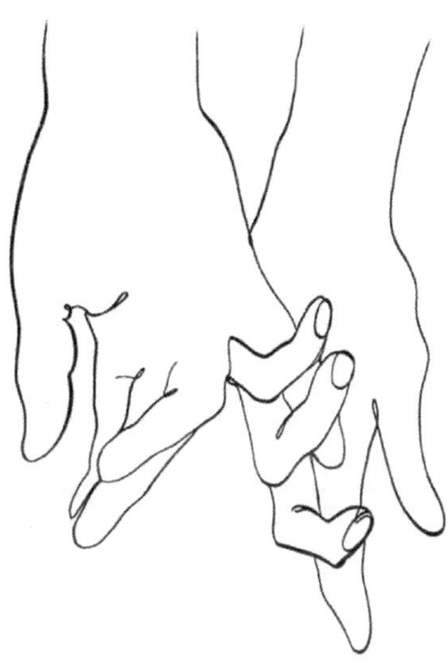

thoughts in my latte

i sat alone with my thoughts in a coffee shop

i stared at my latte as if i were looking for answers

i don't know what it was that i was looking for, but whatever it was wasn't there

after all
it was only a latte

just let it be

i used to be afraid that my writing would come
off as mediocre

i'd get mad when the thoughts in my head
wouldn't map out on paper
and the pages stayed blank

for i knew my mind was on a constant rotation
of thoughts
of ideas
of memories
mistakes
what ifs and maybes

you see, i've always been a hoarder of emotions
i never learned to let things go

constantly rewatering dead plants
i have an entire terrarium of wilting flowers
inside of me

an entire graveyard of different versions of
myself that once was and graves that are
patiently waiting for a new version to acquire
and join as time continues to past

it's funny how things work

the pressure i put on myself to do the one thing
that sets me free

the constant worry about my grammar
my pronunciation
punctuation
and overall potential

or maybe it's just yet another form of projection,
and my self-doubt and own insecurities have put
thoughts of mistrust in my mind, leaving me to
question my overall ability to do even something
as simple as expressing the things i feel

maybe this is yet another way that i have
unconsciously attached myself to the concept of
perfection

but somewhere down the line i've learned that
poetry doesn't care

it's freeing
doesn't abide by specific rules
it lets you be you

poetry helps mistakes look like art

like meaningful, beautiful mistakes

poetry has depth
a sense of rawness, if you will

it is deep
chaotic
captivating
and draws you in all at once

and i believe that people can be poetry too

and i suppose i'd like to believe that one day i,
too, could be considered poetry

we're only human

we are human
 and being human comes with having emotions
we're quite literally meant and designed to feel
and sometimes that's easier said than done

some days the emotions can be joyous and bring
smiles to our faces and on others we're left in
devastation as we reminisce on what once was

i think at some point
somewhere down the line
i've realized that sometimes all you can do is
just sit there

sit there with those emotions and just let them be
what they are
feel them for what they may be and just simply
feel

but there's no reason either of us should have to
sit with our thoughts in solitude

so if you find that your mind is an anchor
weighing you down and you've gotten tired of
wearing the title of the strong one and wish to

just rip it from your sleeve and for once be
vulnerable

i will be there

we can sit together and let the moment be
whatever it needs to be

together we will sit there with the emotions and
just let them be present

after all,
we're only human

my reintroduction

i often overthink

a typical occurrence i've grown accustomed to
somewhere down the line, but lately, i've
wondered who i might be

who i am
who i could be
who i want to be
who i should be
and who they want me to be

am i that little girl who sat quietly on the carpet
of her kindergarten class as she anxiously stayed
quiet while the rest continued to laugh

or am i that girl they made fun of in middle
school when suddenly my looks changed and my
confidence lowered

what about the girl in high school who was told
she was lazy when her grades began to slack?
whose depression set in as the school boys
shoved her into the bookshelf for the uniform
she wore upon her back

there are so many different versions of myself
that are now lost with time

my mind jumps to all the endless possibilities of
others' opinions, and i wish i didn't feel the need
to have their validation

so allow me to take back my power
to reintroduce myself

i am the girl who grew up in chaos but wished to
bring peace to those around her

the girl who looks tenderly after the wounds of
others, not caring about the importance of her
own
a gentle spirit, your sun on your rainy days, and
your moon during the dark

 i am the laughter and the smiles on the faces of
my siblings. i am the daughter who would do
anything to support her parents and finds it an
honor to take care of the ones who have done so
much to help me

i am all the good that was once my grandmother,
for i can only hope to have even half of the
amazing heart and soul that she had

i am dancing in the living room with my
grandfather to his favorite old tunes

i am that little blue house with a front porch and
a big backyard—the one with the small spare
bedroom and memories i'll forever hold onto

 i am the girl who smiles obnoxiously and
sometimes tries to hide it but wishes someone
would tell me i didn't have to

i am the coworker who cares a little too much
about the happiness of those around me and who
will constantly check in, even if unwanted

i am the friend that sometimes lacks
communication but will always be cheering you
on

the girl who looks a little too long into the eyes
of strangers as they pass by, wondering, "what's
their story" and hoping they'll be alright
so i always give an acknowledging smile

i am all of the books i have ever read

all of the poetry i have ever written

i am all of the positive notes that i have left
behind for strangers in random places hoping
that the ones who needed them would find them

i am a calming spirit, a person with which you
can feel at home
the girl you can genuinely and unapologetically
be yourself around

i am all of the handwritten notes that i have ever
been given, and still, i have kept

i am putting my feet up when crossing the
railroad tracks because when i was younger, my
grandfather told me it was good luck

i am all of the names i have spoken when
passing through a cemetery because my mind
tells me that reading them out loud is a way to
bring light and awareness to their name and that
you never know how long it's been since
someone has come to visit

i am all of my childhood stuffed animals that are
softly on display

i am the girl who often dreams about the mother
she'll one day be and the unbelievable amount of
love that she'll have for her babies

i am the girl who sleeps with her feet tucked in
because her sleep paralysis tells her that if she
doesn't, then she might get dragged out of bed

i am the girl who organizes and cleans the tables
at restaurants to leave less work for those who
have served us

the one who won't speak up if an order is wrong
because, who knows, they may be having a
rough day

the girl who uses pinky promises as a valid
means of trust
the one who tends to ramble and mess up her
words

i am the girl who hates small talk and loves to
dive in deep
a hopeless romantic who wears her heart on her
sleeve

i am all of these things and more
all combined into one

i am many things
and i see now that, most importantly
i have always been enough

peace in gratitude

today i was asked a question:

'how do you stay so happy and positive all the time?'

i couldn't help but take a moment to myself and just laugh

me, happy and positive all the time?
if only they knew

i took a moment to think before giving any response

my response
was that i'm not

i'm not always this happy-go-lucky and positive persona that i choose to show

i have my days, weeks, and even months where nothing seems to be okay

but i am thankful

i am thankful for the roof over my head
for my family and my friends

i am thankful for poetry
for music
and for art

and for every single night, i've been blessed to
look up at a sky full of stars

every sunset and sunrise chase
every love and even heartbreak
every dandelion i've ever wished upon

i am thankful for many simple things in life,
things that, to me, are not always as simple as
they seem

i, like any other, have my dark times

but you see, i've learned to overlook those
struggles

i just replace them with gratitude